Action Art

Making Collage

Isabel Thomas

Heinemann Library
Chicago, Illinois

Customer Service   888-454-2279

Visit our website at www.heinemannlibrary.com

Printed and bound in China by South China Printing Company Limited
Photo research by Mica Brancic

09 08 07 06 05
10 9 8 7 6 5 4 3 2 1

Library of Congress Cataloging-in-Publication Data
Thomas, Isabel, 1980-
   Action art : making collage / Isabel Thomas.
       p. cm. -- (Action art)
   Includes bibliographical references and index.
   ISBN 1-4034-6922-9 (library binding-hardcover) -- ISBN 1-4034-6928-8 (pbk.)
   1. Collage--Juvenile literature. I. Title. II. Series.
   TT910.T45 2005
   702'.81'2--dc22
                                                            2005001581

Acknowledgments
The author and publishers are grateful to the following for permission to reproduce
copyright material: Corbis p. **5**; Getty p. **7** (The Image Bank); Harcourt Education pp. **4**,
6, **9**, **10**, **11**, **12**, **13**, **14**, **15**, **16**, **17**, **18**, **19**, **20**, **21**, **22**, **23**, **24**, (Tudor Photography);
Topfoto p. **8** (The Image Works)

Cover photograph of collage reproduced with permission of Harcourt Education
(Tudor Photography).

Every effort has been made to contact copyright holders of any material reproduced in
this book. Any omissions will be rectified in subsequent printings if notice is given to
the publisher.

Many thanks to the teachers, library media specialists, reading instructors, and educational
consultants who have helped develop the Read and Learn/Lee y aprende brand.

Some words are shown in bold, **like this.** You can
find them in the picture glossary on page 23.

Contents

What Is Art?

Art is something you make when you are being **creative**.

People like to look at art.

A person who makes art is called an artist.

You can be an artist, too!

How Can
I Create Art?

There are lots of ways to
create art.

You can draw and paint pictures.

You can make colorful sculptures and prints.

Collage is another kind of art.

What Is Collage?

Collage is making pictures by sticking different things on to paper or cardboard.

Look at all the **materials** you
can use to make collage.

How Do
I Make Collage?

Collect the **materials** that you want to use.

Cut big things into smaller pieces.

brush

glue

You can cut out shapes, too.

Use dabs of glue to stick the materials down.

What Can I Use to Make Collage?

You can tear paper into pieces.

Fold or scrunch the paper to give it **texture**.

Make collage with things that get thrown away.

You can **recycle** old **materials**.

What Else Can I Use to Make Collage?

Fabric collage is nice to touch.

Cotton balls feel soft and fluffy.

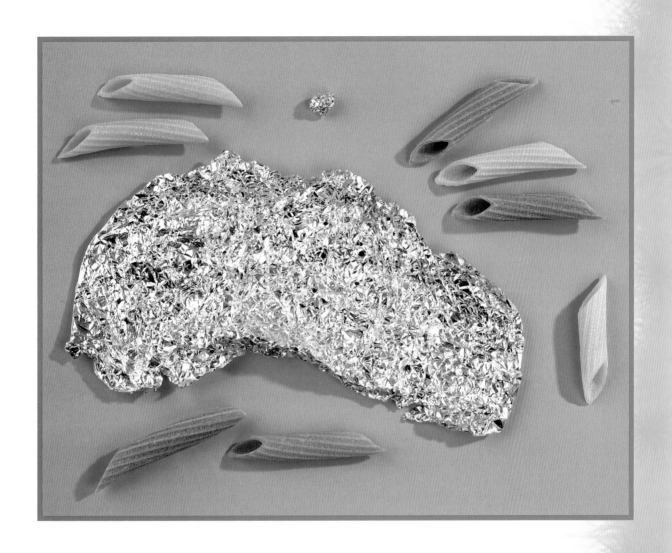

Look for art **materials** in
the kitchen!

Try making collage with shiny
foil and pasta shapes.

What Pictures Can I Make with Collage?

cotton balls

leaves

paper

You can make a picture of something real.

This boy is making a collage of a garden.

You can make up shapes
and patterns.

This is called a design.

How Does Collage Make Me Feel?

When you **display** your collage, you feel proud.

It is fun to talk about collage.

Say what the different **textures** feel like.

Let's Make a Collage!

Let's make a snake collage!

1. Collect **materials** that look and feel interesting.

2. Cut fabric and paper into small pieces.

3. Draw the shape of a snake on a piece of cardboard. Draw stripes on the body.

4. Dab glue on to the first stripe. Stick on pieces of material.

5. Fill in each stripe with something different. Add eyes and a tongue, too.

21

Quiz

Look at these **materials**.

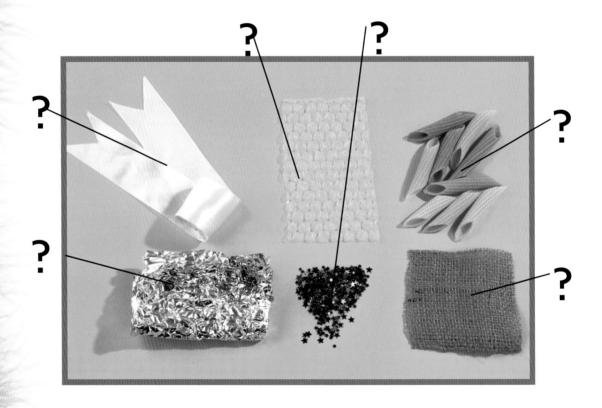

Which ones feel rough? Which ones feel smooth?

Look for the answers on page 24.

Picture Glossary

creative, page 4
making something using your own ideas
and how you feel inside

display, page 18
put your art where other people can
look at it

material, page 9, 10, 13, 15, 20, 22
thing you use to make art

recycle, page 13
use something that would be
thrown away

texture, page 12, 19
how something feels when you touch it

Note to Parents and Teachers

Reading for information is an important part of a child's literacy development. Learning begins with a question about something. Help children think of themselves as investigators and researchers by encouraging their questions about the world around them. Each chapter in this book begins with a question. Read the question together. Look at the pictures. Talk about what you think the answer might be. Then read the text to find out if your predictions were correct. Think of other questions you could ask about the topic, and discuss where you might find the answers. Assist children in using the picture glossary and the index to practice new vocabulary and research skills.

Index

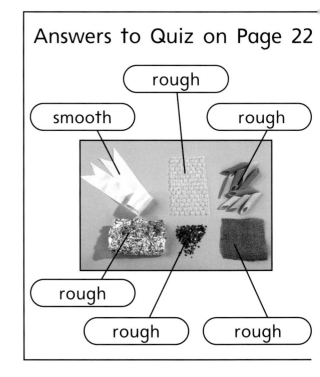

Answers to Quiz on Page 22

rough

smooth

rough

rough

rough

rough